How to Make Money: Selling Inventory Online

Prologue

With the birth of the internet, lifestyle as we once knew it has changed forever. People can now interact with one another, purchase products, watch videos and listen to music all by using a computer connected to the internet. As the internet grow in popularity, more people become accustomed to its use and thus more comfortable with using it in every facet of their lives. Now, the internet is widely used by lots of people as a large source of income! With the birth of EBay, consumers are able to make purchases from the comfort of their own home, having that purchase show up at their door step only days after they had placed their order. Millions and millions of people now turn to online market places such as Ebay, Amazon, Kijiji or Craigslist for their consumption needs. Could you imagine having a store with millions of customers under your roof at a time browsing the products you have for sale? The immergences of online markets have made this possible! People can and DO sell lots and lots of goods simply by listing them up for sale on an online market place; no store rental fees, no large expensive inventory holding space, yet all the benefits of having   products available to millions of people!

I had started using online markets sometime during my first year of university. At the time I had a full course load and a part time job, so in some of my spare time I would list items for sale on the local classifieds sites. It took me a whole couple hours to become familiar with the selling platform of my choice, but after that it was SO EASY! Being a student myself and having to spend hours upon hours reading books, I know how boring it can get. It is for that reason that I have chosen to condense all the information I know into the shortest book possible. This way you will be equipped with the knowledge of this new business system, and be ready to start your new venture in less than one hour! Unlike my last Guide to Making Money "Running Your Own Aeration Business" this business is not seasonal and can be operated all year round! Throughout the content of this book I will be explaining in great detail how to make LARGE amounts of money selling products on online selling platforms such as Kijiji or Craigslist. I will be explaining various "secret" sources of inventory you can use to obtain your items that virtually no one knows about or utilizes! I will also go through the methods you should use to do market research on various items and how to price your items accordingly.

Introduction

If you have ever tried "surfing the web" I am sure you are aware of the hundreds of online "money making scams." Those various pop ups you get claiming that "you can make $100 in under an hour!" Or "Secret work from home business that generates you

$1000 a day!" Before you continue reading my book I would like to ensure you that this is not one of those "get rich quick schemes. It does not require you to give me any start up fees and there is not any hidden "up-sells" coming later in this book. This business is 100% legit and the amount of money you make is directly related to the amount of effort you put into building your business! You may chose to invest as little or as much money into your business as you please, my job is not to manage your funds, my job is to teach you the system that I have used to make money online, and inform you of all the tools that I have used to do so! I do not want to waste anymore time introducing you to my book so without any further a due, here is your new business venture!

Business in a Nutshell

Throughout the duration of this book, you will be taught the simple yet effective methods that I use to obtain and sell inventory on online selling platforms such as Kijiji or Craigslist. By following the simple steps discussed in this book you will become knowledgeable of the BEST sources of inventory, and how to sell it online to make huge profits! While in university I found myself involved in this business and was able to make a large amount of cash by simply buying products from one source and selling them online for a higher price. Basically, you will be acting as a "middleman" buying from one source and moving it to another. The good thing about this business it that it requires minimal labor, unlike the business discussed in my previous book "Running Your Own Aeration Business" which was very labor intensive. Not only does it not require much physical work but it also does not require a whole lot of time. You can simply obtain your items from the sources I am going to soon discuss, and post them on your selling platform in only a matter of a couple hours! The great thing about this is that you can still work your day job, with enough time in your evenings to easily run this business and still have enough time to do the things that you enjoy doing!

For the purpose of making this book easy to follow, I have divided it into sections; I will firstly explain how to use a couple of selling platforms, focusing on those I am most familiar with (Kijiji and Craigslist). After explaining the basic usage of these websites I will dive into the sources you need to be familiar with when obtaining your inventory. Once I teach you where to look for your items, I will teach you what items you should be looking for, how to know exactly which items will sell one hundred percent of the time! I will even go over useful tricks on how to price your items accordingly. I will also include some unique tips that I have learnt while operating this business and some real life examples from my life where I had been successful in selling online! So just to summarize, the rest of the book will read as follows:

1. **Selling Platforms**

2. **Sources of Inventory**

3. **How to Pick Your Items**

4. **Pricing Your Items**

5. **The After Sale Process**

6. **Conclusion**

Selling Platforms

Kijiji

The great thing about this website is its simplicity; it is so easy to use! Here I will briefly go over how to set up an account on this website, and list items. I will not go over every single little detail about this site, I will provide you with enough information to allow you to list your items for sale, and sell them with ease! This will include information on; setting up an account, uploading pictures making your ad and submitting it so it can be viewed by everyone on this website!

Before being able to list any items, you will have to set up an account. This can be done in literally ten minutes, and can be done by clicking the "register now" button in the upper right hand corner of the homepage. After you have filled out some basic information and your account is created you can start to post ads, this can be done by clicking on the "post ad" tab in the upper right hand corner.

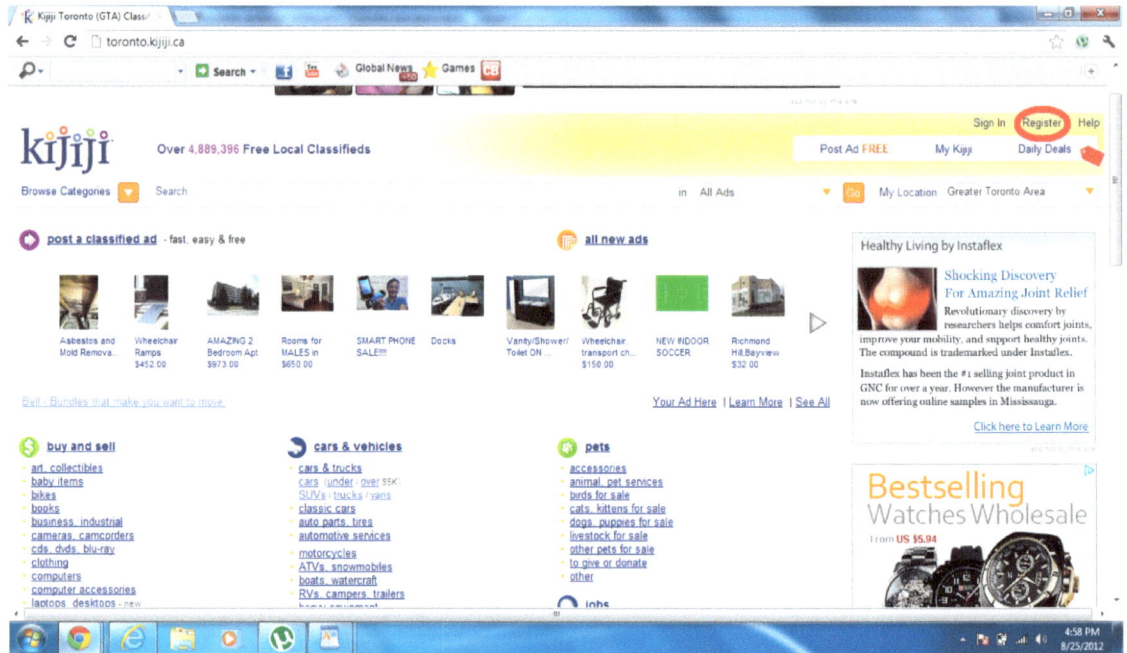

Creating an ad in Kijiji is very simple! You can upload pictures of your item to showcase it to your potential customers, and write a short description about the item you are selling. You should play around with the font style, size and color to make your ad stand out among the others. The better looking the ad, the more likely it is that your item will sell! Once your ad description is all done, you can set your preferred price. There should be some marketing research done before setting the price of your item, I will go more into that in a later section of this book.

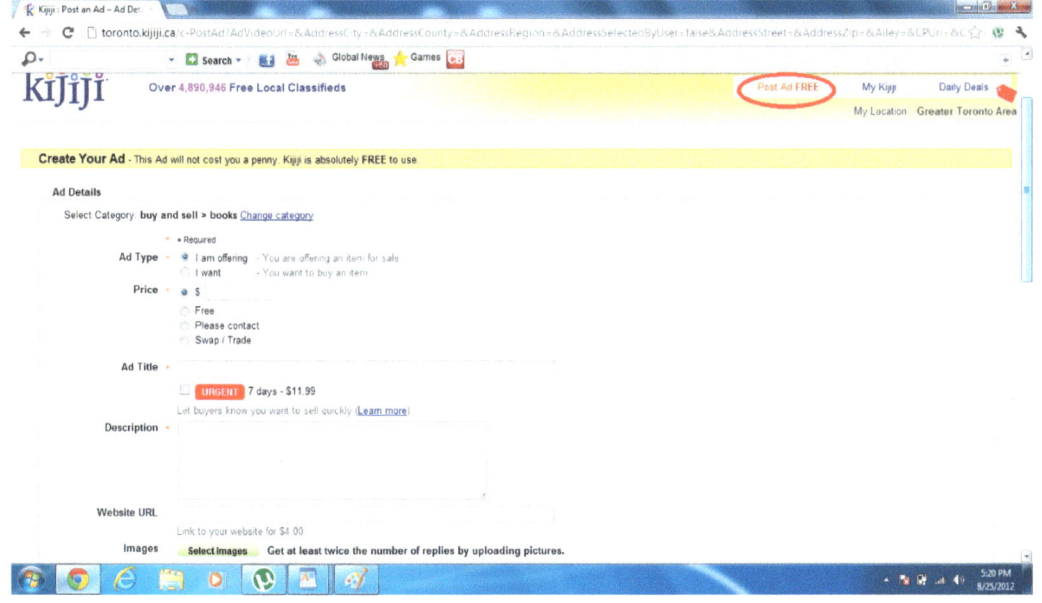

Another tab that you want to take advantage is "browse categories" on the left

hand side of the homepage. Here you can view the ads that other sellers have posted in

all the different categories (cars, books, appliances, toys etc). You can use this to look for

similar items to yours and compare your price, the quality of your ad, and how many

views the ad has! If the ad has a lot of views, most likely it is a popular item and will sell. A

more useful tab under "browse categories" is the "wanted ads" tab.   Here you can

examine the exact items that people are looking for. When looking for inventory, you

keep these people in mind and contact them when you have found something they may

be interested in. Later on in the book I will explain a method I used to set up a sale before

spending a single dollar on any inventory!

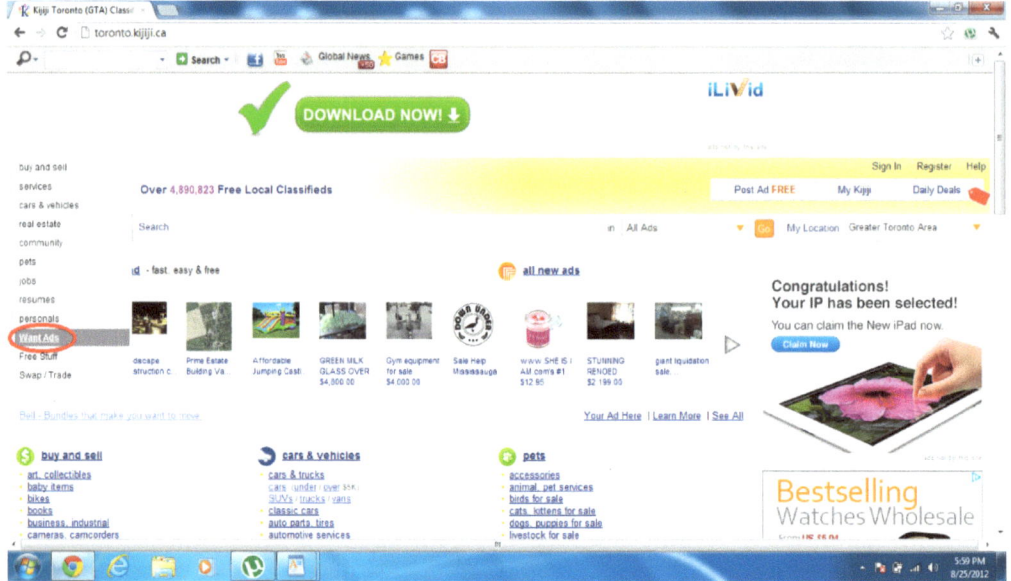

I did not use many more of the features on the website. Everything I have gone over thus far had been enough to keep me busy and the sales consistent. I am aware of certain "up sells" on the website that make it easier for your ad to get views. These consist of paying a certain amount of money to have your ad appear on the homepage, or having it at the top of its category. Like I said, I did not use these features at all, I never needed to pay any fees to have my items sell, so I will not put anymore space into talking about it rather than saying, you have the option to do so.

So there you have it, your first selling platform explained enough to get you started with selling your inventory. Everything I went over about kijiji will be needed when selling items online. It should not take you long to get a hang of using this site, I feel like it is the easiest one to use, and one with the best layout! Take some time to go over everything I explained and by the time you are listing your first item, it will take no more than 5 minutes!

Craigslist

Craigslist is yet another online classified website similar to Kijiji. I feel that

Craigslist has been around longer and may be a little bit more popular. I won't spend too

much time going over this platform because it is very similar to Kijiji in respect to the

layout and registration. One difference about Craigslist has to do with the ad maker; you

have the option to use html coding to make your ad stand out. I will go over an easy way

to make your ad look slick, which should help you with your sales.

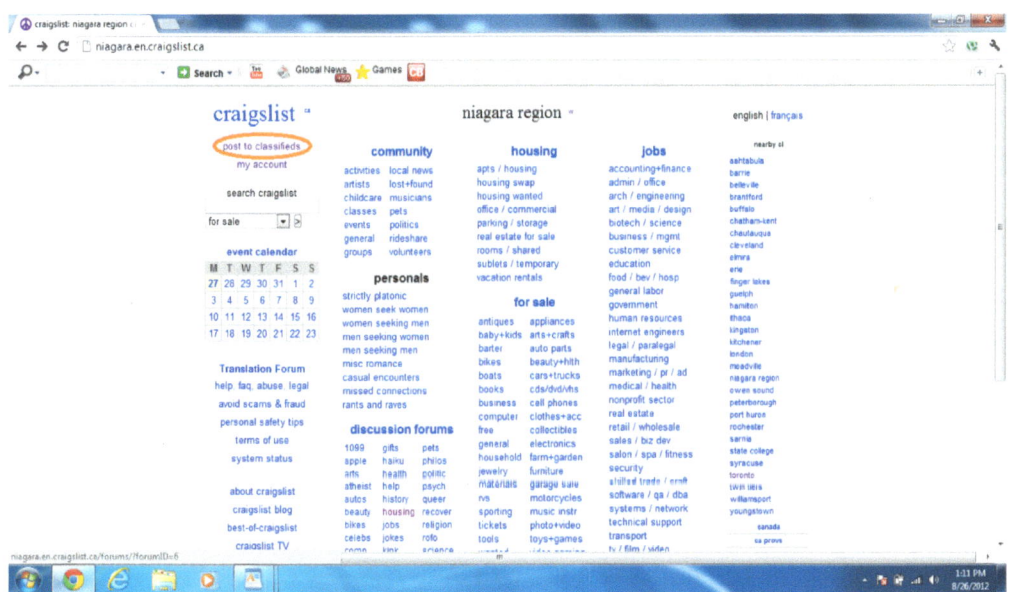

So here you have the homepage of Craigslist. As you can see, it is not as visually appealing as Kijiji, but more or less does the same thing. In the top left hand corner you

have the option of registering for an account and also posting an ad to the classifieds. Like

I said I do not want to go over very much about this website because it is very similar to

Kijiji.

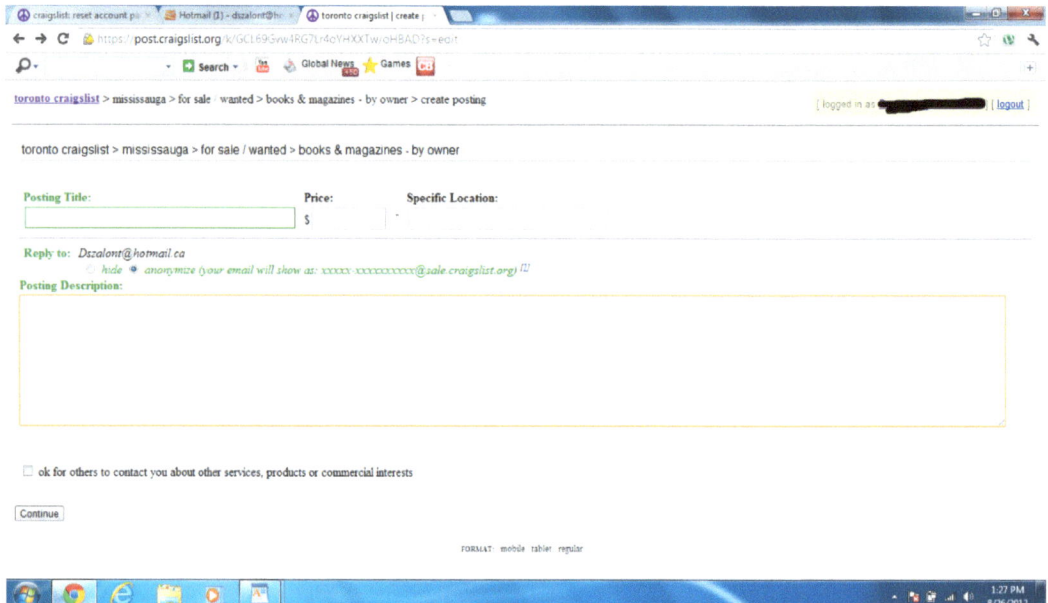

Here you have the ad posting outline for Craigslist. As you can see, very similar to

Kijiji, just put the title of your item, chose price and write a summary description about

the item you are selling. There is not much more to explain, I feel like you will not have

any problems figuring the rest of this website out!

Sources of Inventory

When looking for a steady supply of merchandise to sell I came across numerous sources, all of which had proven successful. Finding these did not happen overnight, in fact it took a lot of research and networking to come up with these sources. Luckily for you I will save you the hassle and time of trying to find out where to find them and list them all HERE, in this book! Be grateful!

Liquidation Auctions

Liquidation auctions are very useful when it comes to finding items to sell online! Usually held once a week in a warehouse, these places gather misguided freight, over stalked goods from retail, unclaimed luggage from airports and items seized by the police and auction them off to the public for a fraction of retail value! Most of these liquidation companies post pictures of the items they are auctioning a couple nights before the auction. This allows you to browse through the inventory and make note of anything you feel would likely sell online! It helps to have a pen and paper to write down the item so you can do some research about it before attending the auction.

Something very important to remember about these auctions is that usually they hold a 10% premium charge on anything sold plus any applicable taxes, you need to keep this in mind when placing your bids. Be smart, most people shop online looking for deals so make sure you purchase the good at a price (including the premium charge and tax) in which you can turn a profit AND offer your potential online customers a reasonable deal. You should bring a notepad with you that has the list of items you wish to bid on (you decided on these by browsing the auction pictures). You should also have pricing information on each of these items (what they go for retail, what you have seen them go for on other online sites). This allows you to know your limit when bidding on items, the price should be substantially LOWER than any retail price of the same item!

Like I said earlier in this book, I will be giving real life examples from my experience with this business, to show you that this really works! Here is an example of an item that I was able to pick up from a liquidation auction and sell it quickly to make some EASY CASH:

I remember one night at the auction, there was an abundance of pet products. Doing my research the night before, I felt that I would be successful getting my hands on two different products. One of the items was Dog paw wipes; I felt that this would be an easy item to sell on Kijiji, an item that truly sells itself! "You take your shoes off after walking outside to keep bacteria from entering your home, your dogs paws should be clean to prevent the same spread of bacteria" a perfect pitch! The other item were these collars for dogs that kills fleas, I remember doing research on the product, it was selling retail for $15.00, I thought selling for $10.00 cash would be enough of a deal to make people want to buy at the auction I ended up getting over-bid on the paw wipes, but had managed to pick up a pack of 24 flea-collars for only $11.00 including tax and buyers premium! One sale alone would cover the cost of my investment.

I went home that night, put together an ad on Kijiji and went to bed. Within the next couple days I had sold 10 of these dog collars, some customers buying multiple items at a time! In a weeks time all collars were sold, and I profited $230 from doing barely any work! This was the profit off of one buy and one auction! Buying numerous items and attending multiple auctions allowed me to bring in an extra $1,000 dollars in cash!

It obviously helps to grab more than one item when attending these auctions, seeing that the time you spend going to these auctions should be factored into your profit margin. The more items that you pick up from the auction, the more listings you will have on your selling platform therefore increasing your sales and your profit!

In order to find these auctions close to your place of residence, a simple Google search is suffice. Just type in "liquidation auction" and the area in which you live to find a source.   Once you find one of these auctions, finding more is a walk in the park. When you attend the auction get acquainted with the other people there, most likely they have been there before and can help you with finding more auctions in the immediate area!

I am going to end this section by listing the auctions that I attend. These are all located within the Greater Toronto Area and may not be of any relevance to you. It may still be beneficial for you to check out the websites of these auctions to see what type of items they have for sale!

http://www.principalliquidators.com/

http://kcauctions.ca/

http://rightbidauctions.com/

Antique Stores

Antique stores happen to be my favorite source of inventory! They are the perfect place to find those one of a kind items that people will pay BIG BUCKS for. Most of my highest mark-up items have come from antique stores and if you think about it, it makes a lot of sense. Usually antiques appeal to a certain group of people, or a single collector; if you take that one item and place it online so that now millions of people can see it, the chances of finding that collector increases dramatically.

When buying from antique stores, you want to locate ones in smaller towns; I find that ones in the cities and highly populated areas jack the prices because they know that people living in the city can afford to pay these prices. Go to stores in more remote areas, usually the items found here are gathered from garage sales, or if someone has passed away, items from their house are sometimes bought from the dealer and sold in their store.

Although I had found and sold A LOT of items from this source, my selling process differed from that of the liquidation auctions. Remember earlier in the book when I discussed the "wanted" ads folder in Kijiji (you can do this in Craigslist as well)? This is where that tab comes handy! Before heading over to the antique store, I would browse through the wanted ad section and see what people were demanding. Usually there were at least 10 people looking for some type of collectable good. I would write down everything they were looking for and head over to the antique store to see if there was anything that would cater to their needs. Nine out of ten times I would find at least one item I could sell to these buyers!

I had found and sold all sorts of items from antique stores; old post cards, toys, military memorabilia, signs, mugs, posters, coke memorabilia, books and much more! I am going to share with you one successful sale I had made, selling an item I had purchased from an antique store:

Searching the Kijiji "wanted" ads I came across a collector of signs seeking out license plates. In the ad i remember it saying that she was making a room with walls covered in various road signs and plates. I took note of it on my iPad and walked to the local antique store. It just so happened that there was a HUGE pile of license plates on one of the shelves, over 100 of them! It helps to bring some form of smart phone or tablet with you so that you can take pictures and send them to your potential buyers, or your own email. I had taken pictures of the license plates and attached to an email stating that I had *found a bunch of license plates and was wondering if she was interested. I walked over to the nearby coffee shop to finish up some homework, and during that time, I had received an email from the collector stating she was very interested. When asking about pricing, we negotiated a deal of 6 dollars a plate, and she was going to drive to meet me in town. I quickly went back to the antique store, and asked the owner how much he was selling the plates for. Turns out he was selling them for $3.00 a piece! A very high profit margin still, but I knew I could get them lower because I was going to buy them all. I managed to get him down to $2.00 a piece. I spent $200 on the plates, but managed to sell them for $600, a profit of $400!*

You should not limit yourself to one antique store, for the same reason that you should not limit yourself to one liquidation auction; the more items you can find to sell, the larger your profit margin will be! A simple Google search will let you know of any antique stores within your preferred area. You could also ask people you see in an antique store for the location of others and soon enough you will be equipped with enough sources to keep your inventory strong and your sales high!

Over-Seas Suppliers

Using overseas suppliers can be very profitable if you are thinking of selling in large quantities. Personally I have not used this method of obtaining inventory a whole lot, but know enough to inform you about them. The only overseas wholesale website I have ever bought from has been Alibaba

At this website you are connected to hundreds of Chinese manufacturers who offer just about anything at wholesale price! Like I said I have not used this source very often, but when I did, I had some research done prior to my buying. When selling on online classified websites take a look at some hot items on eBay. You can do this by searching an item and checking the completed listings. If you notice an item is selling frequently, go over to alibaba and search that item. Chances are you will find multiple supplier of that exact item! The truth is that a lot of people selling items on eBay actually obtain them from this exact website, and for a fraction of the price they are listed on eBay for! Usually you have to order items from this website in large quantities, but if you ask the supplier for a "sample shipment" you should be able to receive a smaller quantity.

A personal experience with this website had gone especially good:

A friend and I had ordered these glow in the dark iPhone cases and they sold like *hotcakes on eBay and Kijiji! Before I bought this item, I had checked it out on eBay and it seemed to have been doing quite well. I ordered a sample from alibaba of about 100 items and then listed my ad on Kijiji and eBay. Within about a week all 100 were sold for $12.00 each and they were bought for $1.20! HUGE profit.*

How to Pick Your Items

So now you know multiple places to obtain your inventory and multiple places to sell it. Now it is time for me to give you a few pointers on how to pick your items to list. There is in fact a very useful tip that not many sellers are aware of that I use to make sure my items sell each and every time! Head on over to the Ebay website. I didn't go over selling on this website because there are many books out there on Ebay alone, and with shipping and listing fees I thought it would be easier to stick to online local classifieds! Just because you will not be selling on eBay does not mean you can't use it as a very helpful tool. I happen to use Ebay to see what is hot in the market and buy my items accordingly. You may be wondering how I used Ebay to find these items and the truth is, it is very easy. On eBay when searching for an item you have the option of doing an "advanced search".

For an example, I made a search for "Halloween props" , a good seasonal line of items to sell. As shown circled in red, there is an option to do an advanced search. Clicking on that button gives you a lot of different choices so you can narrow down your search. The only two that I would pay any attention to would be; "number of bids" and "completed listings".

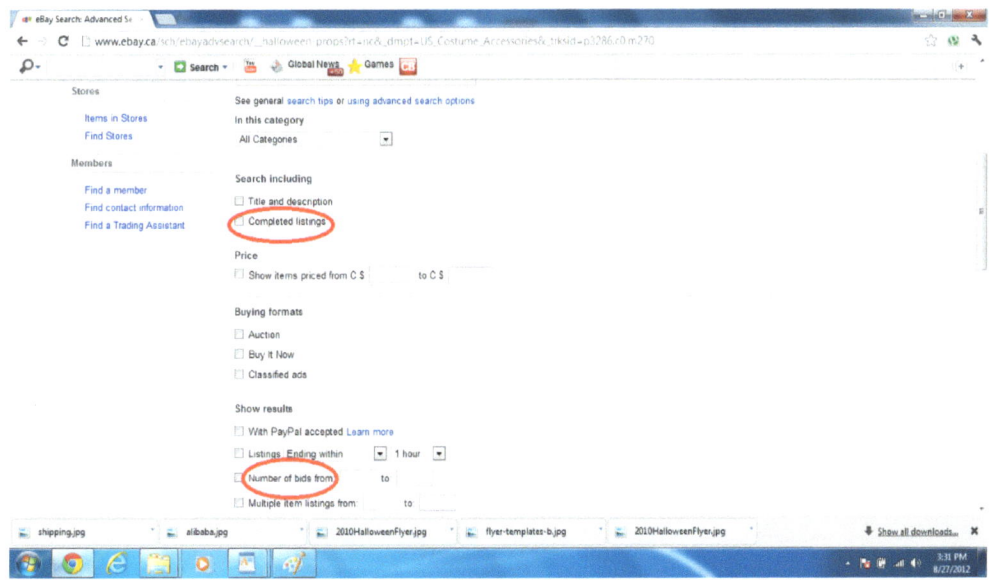

By checking off the completed listing box what happens is that you are shown all the items in the category you searched that either sold or didn't. This is very useful because it shows what items are currently selling. Usually if you see an item that has sold multiple times with a high number of bids on it, it means that the item is in high demand and that you should take note of that, look for it when you are at an auction or go over to alibaba and see if you can get it ordered. Items with current high number of bids also mean it is in high demand, you should also try and find these in auction, at the antique store or from overseas suppliers.

Pricing Your Item

Pricing your item accordingly is very important when it comes to selling online.

You must understand that people come to shop online in order to save money. You cannot make a sale on an item posting it for more than retail or for more than anywhere else that item may be listed. There are a couple good ways in finding how much you should charge for your listing, and I will go over them in this section.

Remember the liquidation auctions I was telling you about? I hope so. There is in fact a little powerful piece of software you can use at these auctions to find out how to price your items accordingly, it's called red laser.

This little piece of software allows you to scan any barcode and see which stores are selling it and how much it is going for. It even tracks if that item is being sold anywhere online, and the current price it is going for! You can obtain this app for any smart phone, or tablet on the market.

Another method you could use to set the price for your item is doing a price cross analysis with the same or similar item on eBay. This way you will know the online value of your item and will not over or under price it.

The After Sale Process

Okay, so your item has successfully sold on one of the selling platforms discussed above, congratulations! When using online classifieds such as Craigslist and Kijiji, most of the time you do not need to worry about shipping anything! Since your item is advertised to people within your immediate location, you can usually agree upon a meeting place. I would recommend meeting in a public place, in seeing that you do not totally know who this person is, and somewhere close by in walking distance from your place of residence in seeing that costs of transportation cut into your profit margin! Getting your item to your customer is not a complicated process since usually you have already exchanged contact information with your customer (phone number and email) and can easily arrange a time and place that fits both your schedules.

If the rare occasion happens and your buyer wants you to ship the item, do not panic! This is a very easy process. I remember the first time I had to ship an item and I was worried at first. I went over to the postal office with the item in one hand, and a piece of paper with the address of my customer in the other. The postal office worker was very helpful and guided me through the process. All you need to do is have the address you are shipping to and the item in a secure package so it does not break while being shipped. If you do not have anything to put the item in, they can take care of it for you at the postal office. To make the payment go as smooth as possible I advise you to open up a PayPal account or activate internet banking on your bank account. REMEMBER to include shipping and handling into your price. If you do not, then your profit margin decreases the amount that you spent on packaging and shipping the item.

A very useful tactic to use when delivering your products, whether it be in person or by shipping, is to include some sort of reference so your buyers can keep in contact with you. What I did was make a business card with my selling platform account name, and a title "thank you for purchasing" with a subtitle "make sure to check out my other items for sale!" This way one of your customers who have bought from you in the past can keep in touch and buy from you again! You have already built up the seller/buyer trust which is key when selling online; you might as well take advantage of it!

Conclusion

Well there you have it, all the information you need to start selling items on your online classifieds website! It took me a long time to learn everything that I have shared with you in this book, having all this information within less than an hour should be a game changer for the success of your business! I know that with a little bit of hard work and some effort on your part in executing this business you will be able to see great results! Using all the resources I have talked about in this book is more than enough to get you started. Whether you are looking for a new job or just some supplementary income to help pay the bills, this business will help you get there. So what are you waiting for? Go make your selling platform account and start looking for those inventory sources!

Do not forget to read about my other business ventures!

How to Make Money: Running Your Own Aeration Business

How to Make Money: Using Fiverr.com

If you have any questions regarding the business or future business endeavors, do not hesitate to contact me at davesbizbooks@gmail.com

Thank you for reading,

www.ingramcontent.com/pod-product-compliance
Lightning Source LLC
Chambersburg PA
CBHW050911180526
45159CB00007B/2873